Readin Speed & Content

Grades 4-5

REM 1042

A TEACHING RESOURCE FROM

REMEDIA PUBLICATIONS

©2021, 2019, 2015, 2009, 1980
Copyright by Remedia Publications, Inc.
All Rights Reserved. Printed in the U.S.A.

The purchase of this product entitles the individual teacher to reproduce copies for classroom use. The reproduction of any part for an entire school or school system is strictly prohibited.

www.rempub.com

REMEDIA PUBLICATIONS, INC.
SCOTTSDALE, AZ

This product utilizes innovative strategies and proven methods to improve student learning. The product is based upon reliable research and effective practices that have been replicated in classrooms across the United States. Information regarding the Common Core State Standards this product meets is available at www.rempub.com/standards

INTRODUCTION

Reading for Speed & Content is designed to exercise and build several reading skills. The topics were chosen for their high interest appeal and most address nonfiction subjects. Each activity consists of four sections:

Vocabulary: Before reading, students review words they will come across as they read and use them in sentences to assure understanding of meanings.

Reading: Stories vary from approximately 100-400 words in length and are ordered according to reading level difficulty (based on a combination of vocabulary difficulty, word length, and sentence length) from easiest to hardest. They may be used as timed reading exercises if you choose.

Comprehension: Each story is followed by several comprehension questions.

Cloze Reading: A full page of cloze (fill-in-the-blank) sentences test comprehension and the ability to use context clues to choose the correct word.

An Answer Key has been provided for your use. Students should be encouraged to use complete sentences for answers.

If stories are used to develop students' reading speed, there are two options:

1. Have students read the entire story. Keep track of the amount of time this takes (minutes and seconds).

    Have them enter their time and number of words read in the spaces provided at the end of each story. Use these figures to find words per minute on the *Timed Reading Chart* (see pg. 43).

2. Set a time limit for reading the story. Stop the students when the time is up.

    Have them enter the number of words read and the time in the spaces provided. Use the figures to find words per minute on the Chart.

Word counts are provided at the end of every line in the story so that the number of words read can be determined quickly and easily. A *Keeping Track* record sheet is included so students may see their improvement in reading rate.

Stories may be reproduced for use with groups of any size or as independent exercises.

CONTENTS

Chewing Gum	1-3
Band-Aids	4-6
Kids' Railroad	7-9
Think Ink	10-12
Fad Fun	13-15
Holidays	16-18
Funny Fashions	19-21
Sports Cards	22-24
Film Facts	25-27
Food for Thought	28-30
A Castle Fit for a Vampire	31-33
Smokey the Bear	34-36
Amazing Artists	37-39
Teddy Bears	40-42
Timed Reading Chart	43
Keeping Track	44
Answer Key	45

Name _____   **Chewing Gum**

WORDS TO KNOW

chicle	chic • le	sap	sap
flavorings	fla • vor • ings	rubbery	rub • ber • y
inventor	in • vent • or	sapodilla	sap • o • dil • la
machine	ma • chine	shopkeeper	shop • keep • er
package	pack • age	tacos	ta • cos

Chewing Gum

Did you ever wonder how chewing gum came to be? — 10

The first chewing gum was nothing more than a lump of chicle. — 22
Chicle is a rubbery sap that comes from a tree. The tree is the sapodilla — 37
and grows in Mexico. For hundreds of years the Mexican people had — 49
chewed chicle. — 51

Then an American inventor, Thomas Adams, found a large wad of — 62
chicle. He thought it was very interesting. He first tried to heat it and — 76
make it into a new kind of rubber. That didn't work. — 87

Next he tried to use it to make false teeth stay in people's mouths. — 101
That didn't work very well either. Finally he boiled it and rolled it out flat — 116
with a rolling pin. He would break off little pieces to chew. — 128

He sold his "chewing gum" in a candy store in New Jersey. Everyone — 141
loved it! Mr. Adams then made the first gum-making machine. His — 153
machine would mix chicle, flavorings, and sugar. Then it would roll it out — 166
into flat sheets. — 169

Shopkeepers bought the gum in these big pieces. When someone — 179
wanted a penny's worth of gum, the shopkeeper would break off a piece. — 192

Soon other companies began making chewing gum. They added — 201
new flavors and bright packages. Just before the year 1900, William — 212
Wrigley Jr. began making chewing gum. He spent more money on ads for — 225
his gum than any other company. Soon he was selling more gum than all — 239
the others. — 241

In 1914, people in America were chewing about 39 sticks of gum — 253
each year. By 1925, the average number was up to 100 sticks for each — 267

(Continued on next page)

Name _____ **Chewing Gum**

(Continued)

person in one year. Now it is much higher than that! 278

    Today chewing gum comes in a rainbow of colors. There are many, ... 290
many flavors from which to choose. Gum comes in sticks, balls, and 302
squares. It even comes shaped like tacos, french fries, and hot dogs. You ... 315
can buy gum with sugar or without it! 323

    Gum chewing seems to be one sport that will be around for a long 337
time. 338

WORDS READ	TIME	WORDS PER MINUTE

1. From what is chewing gum made? _____

2. Where do we get chicle? _____

3. Name one thing Thomas Adams tried to make out of chicle, other than gum.
   _____

4. What is added to chicle to make chewing gum better?
   _____

5. How was chewing gum first sold? _____
   _____

6. Why did Mr. Wrigley sell more gum than anyone else? _____
   _____

7. What is your favorite chewing gum flavor? _____

8. Why do you think some people chew gum without sugar? _____
   _____

Reading for Speed & Content – Book 3 ©Remedia Publications

Name _____   *Chewing Gum*

WORDS

America	choose	more	sold
around	colors	tried	would
chewing	companies	Shopkeepers	
Chicle	it		

Fill in the blanks using the words in the box above.

1. The first _____ gum was nothing more than a lump of chicle.

2. _____ is a rubbery sap that comes from a tree.

3. He first _____ to heat it and make it into a new kind of rubber.

4. Finally he boiled _____ and rolled it out flat with a rolling pin.

5. He _____ his "chewing gum" in a candy store in New Jersey.

6. _____ bought the gum in these big pieces.

7. When someone wanted a penny's worth of gum, the shopkeeper _____ break off a piece.

8. Soon other _____ began making chewing gum.

9. He spent _____ money on ads for his gum than any other company.

10. In 1914, people in _____ were chewing about 39 sticks of gum each year.

11. Today chewing gum comes in a rainbow of _____ .

12. There are many, many flavors from which to _____ .

13. Gum chewing seems to be one sport that will be _____ for a long time.

Name _____

Band-Aids

WORDS TO KNOW

accident	ac • ci • dent	company	com • pa • ny
adhesive	ad • he • sive	gauze	gauze
bandages	band • ag • es	plastic	plas • tic
blister	blis • ter	unwind	un • wind

Band-Aids

You cut your finger. What do you do to keep it clean? 12

You fall and scrape your knee. What will keep it from 24
bumped again? 26

Your new shoes made a blister on your heel. What will keep it from 40
hurting? 41

The answer to these questions is put a Band-Aid on it! 53

Did you ever wonder who came up with the idea for Band-Aids? 66

Many years ago, about 1920, a man named Earle Dickson worked 77
for the Johnson and Johnson Company. This company made cloth 87
adhesive tape and gauze to cover cuts and scrapes. 96

Mr. Dickson's young wife, Josephine, was always getting small cuts 106
while doing her housework. Each time it happened she had to cut a small 120
strip of gauze. Then she would fold it to make a pad. She would put the 136
pad over her cut. Then she would have to cut a strip of cloth tape to hold 153
the gauze on. This took lots of time and trouble. 163

One day Mr. Dickson had an idea to help his wife. He made many little 178
pads of gauze. Then he unrolled the tap and stuck the little pads on the tape. 194
He placed them about 4 inches apart. Then he rolled up the tape again. 208

Now when Josephine had an accident she could unwind and cut off 220
a piece. She had ready-made Band-Aids! 228

Mr. Dickson told the people at Johnson and Johnson what he had 240
done. They thought it was a great idea! Soon they made the idea even 254
better. They cut them and put each one in a paper wrapper. 266

In 1958 Johnson and Johnson began making their Band-Aids with 277

(Continued on next page)

Name _____   **Band-Aids**

(Continued)

plastic tape because it stuck better. Very soon other companies followed 288
the idea. They could not use the name Band-Aid because the name 301
belonged to Johnson and Johnson. 306

Now these handy little bandages come in all sizes and shapes and in 319
all colors and designs from Snoopy to Superman. 327

The sticky business of covering cuts and scrapes turns out about 338
4 billion bandages each year. 343

WORDS READ	TIME	WORDS PER MINUTE

1. For what company did Mr. Dickson work? _____

2. Why did Mrs. Dickson need lots of tape and gauze? _____

3. How did Mr. Dickson's idea help his wife? _____

4. Why can't other companies use the name "Band-Aid"? _____

5. How many bandage strips are made in a year? _____

6. What material is now used in Band-Aids instead of cloth tape?

Name _____   **Band-Aids**

WORDS

accident	over	she	what
better	man	thought	wife
had	scrapes	time	wrapper

Fill in the blanks using the words in the box above.

1. Many years ago, about 1920, a _____ named Earle Dickson worked for the Johnson and Johnson Company.

2. Johnson and Johnson made cloth adhesive tape and gauze to cover cuts and _____ .

3. Mr. Dickson's young _____ , Josephine, was always getting small cuts while doing her housework.

4. Each _____ it happened she had to cut a small strip of gauze.

5. Then she would fold it to make a pad to put _____ her cut.

6. Then _____ would have to cut a strip of cloth tape to hold the gauze on.

7. One day Mr. Dickson _____ an idea to help his wife.

8. Now when Josephine had an _____ she could unwind and cut off a piece.

9. Mr. Dickson told the people at Johnson and Johnson _____ he had done.

10. They _____ it was a great idea!

11. Soon they made the idea even better by cutting them and putting each one in a paper _____ .

12. In 1958 Johnson and Johnson began making their Band-Aids with plastic tape because it stuck _____ .

Reading for Speed & Content – Book 3   6   ©Remedia Publications

Name _____

Kids' Railroad

WORDS TO KNOW

Budapest	Bu • da • pest	railway	rail • way
collect	col • lect	station	sta • tion
conductor	con • duc • tor	uniform	u • ni • form
different	dif • fer • ent	unusual	un • u • su • al

Kids' Railroad

Since they were first invented, trains have interested people. You don't have to be a kid to love trains. Lots of adults collect and play with toy trains.

Many children are given toy trains when they are much too young to enjoy them. But Dad sure has a good time!

There is a very unusual train, a real full-sized train in Budapest, Hungary. The reason it is so unusual is that it is run completely by children. It is called the Pioneer Railway.

For over 30 years, children from the ages of 10 to 14 have been running this train. About 700 children work on the railroad. About 50 are on duty at a time. They wear dark blue uniforms with red hats.

They work as station masters, ticket sellers, and conductors. They operate the controls and do all the other jobs to keep the Pioneer Railway on the track.

The train runs back and forth on 7 miles of track. Each year it carries thousands of people in its cars back and forth through the country. The train goes through tunnels, onto side tracks, and into the station at each small town.

Each worker gets a chance to try many different jobs. To be a railway worker on the Pioneer, the young people must do very well in school. Then they must pass tests to make sure they can do the work.

They go to classes for about four months to learn all about running a train. When they are ready they start with some of the easier jobs. As they learn more by watching and helping they are able to do more. The

(Continued on next page)

Name _____   **Kids' Railroad**

(Continued)

workers take their jobs very seriously. They know that they must do their	289
very best each day. People's lives depend on how well they do those jobs.	303
The train has been running for more than thirty years. It runs from	316
early in the morning until late in the evening. And in all that time, the	331
Pioneer Railway has never had an accident!	338

WORDS READ	TIME	WORDS PER MINUTE

1. Why do fathers buy toy trains for very young children? _____
   _____

2. What is the name of the "children's" railroad? _____
   _____

3. How many children are on duty at one time? _____

4. How long is the track? _____

5. Why must the children be very good at their jobs? _____
   _____

6. How long has the railway been running? _____

7. Name two of the criteria young people must meet before they can work there.
   _____
   _____

Name _____   **Kids' Railroad**

WORDS

all	forth	months	seriously
children	invented	play	to
duty	it	sellers	unusual
goes			

Fill in the blanks using the words in the box above.

1. Since they were first _____ , trains have interested people.

2. Lots of adults collect and _____ with toy trains.

3. There is a very _____ train, a real full-sized train in Budapest, Hungary.

4. The Pioneer Railway is run completely by _____ .

5. About 50 children are on _____ at a time.

6. They work as station masters, ticket _____ , and conductors.

7. They operate the controls and do _____ the other jobs to keep the Pioneer Railway on the track.

8. The train runs back and _____ on 7 miles of track.

9. Each year _____ carries thousands of people in its cars back and forth through the country.

10. The train _____ through tunnels, onto side tracks, and into the station at each small town.

11. Each worker gets a chance _____ try many different jobs.

12. They go to classes for about four _____ to learn all about running a train.

13. The workers take their jobs very _____ because they know that people's lives depend on how well they do those jobs.

Name _____   **Think Ink**

WORDS TO KNOW

ballpoint	ball • point	manuscripts	man • u • scripts
chemicals	chem • i • cals	moisture	mois • ture
cuttlefish	cut • tle • fish	preservatives	pre • ser • va • tives
dissolved	dis • solved	refills	re • fills
ingredients	in • gre • di • ents	resisted	re • sist • ed
invention	in • ven • tion	sulfate	sul • fate

Think Ink

The next time you write with your ballpoint pen, think about the ink 13
as it dries on your paper. Ink is a liquid that is mixed with dye to form a 31
color. It has been around in some form for thousands of years. 43

Ink was probably discovered about 4,500 years ago. Egypt and 53
China used it for writing manuscripts about 2,500 B.C. Their ink was 66
made from berries or carbon and water. The Romans made their ink from 79
the cuttlefish. 81

These inks resisted moisture. They have lasted for centuries. By 91
reading what ancient people wrote, we have learned much about their 102
customs. 103

For thousands of years, ink stayed pretty much the same. But the 115
objects used to write with ink changed. Ancient people used sticks or sharp 128
objects. By George Washington's time, people used feather pens, called quills. 139

A major invention was the ballpoint pen in the 1940's. At last, there 152
was a pen that wouldn't run out of ink every few hours. That was the big 168
problem with old-fashioned fountain pens. People had to carry their ink 180
bottles everywhere for quick refills. 185

Today the best inks contain dye and certain acids. They also have 197
chemicals to make the ink last. They are called preservatives. Other 208
ingredients in the ink keep it wet. 215

There are many kinds of ink for all kinds of jobs. Most ink is blue, 230
black, or red. It won't fade, even when it gets wet or light hits it. One kind 247
you might have heard of is India ink. 255

The ballpoint pen uses ink that is as thick as syrup. It contains 268
40% dye, which is a lot. 274

(Continued on next page)

Name _____   ***Think Ink***

(Continued)

    There is even a special printer's ink. It must stay wet a long time, then dry very quickly.   288 / 292

    Invisible ink has been popular for years. It lets you write secret messages. The paper looks blank until the receiver uses heat or light or chemicals to unlock its powers. Then the writing begins to appear. If heat is used, the ink will turn blue on paper.   304 / 317 / 330 / 339

WORDS READ	TIME	WORDS PER MINUTE

1. When was ink probably discovered? _____

2. What two countries were using ink at about the same time long ago? _____

3. Feather pens are also called _____ .

4. What major invention occurred in the 1940's? _____

5. Most inks come in these three colors: _____

6. The fun kind of ink you can't see is: _____

7. If heat is used, invisible ink will turn _____ .

8. Why do you think invisible ink is so popular? _____

Name _____   **Think Ink**

WORDS

ballpoint	Invisible	make	sticks
blue	liquid	red	wrote
had	long	stay	years
ink	major		

Fill in the blanks using the words in the box above.

1. Ink is a _____ that is mixed with dye to form a color.

2. The Romans made their _____ from the cuttlefish.

3. By reading what ancient people _____ , we have learned much about their customs.

4. For thousands of _____ , ink stayed pretty much the same.

5. Ancient people used _____ or sharp objects to write with.

6. A _____ invention was the ballpoint pen in the 1940's.

7. People _____ to carry their ink bottles everywhere for quick refills.

8. They have chemicals to _____ the ink last.

9. Most ink is blue, black, or _____ .

10. Other inks don't last as _____ .

11. The _____ pen uses ink that is as thick as syrup.

12. Printer's ink must _____ wet a long time, then dry very quickly.

13. _____ ink lets you write secret messages.

14. If heat is used the ink will turn _____ on paper.

Reading for Speed & Content – Book 3   12   ©Remedia Publications

Name _____

Fad Fun

WORDS TO KNOW

bamboo	bam • boo	marathon	mar • a • thon
behavior	be • hav • ior	natives	na • tives
contestants	con • tes • tants	occurred	oc • curred
hoisted	hoist • ed	popular	pop • u • lar
hula	hu • la	possessed	pos • sessed

Fad Fun

One day in the 1930's a young student swallowed a live goldfish as a joke. Soon, thousands of college students were trying to see how many they could swallow at one time. There were reports of boys swallowing up to 199 goldfish. It had become a fad.

A fad is a certain kind of behavior that is very popular for a short time. Some other fads were tie dye t-shirts, pet rocks, and beanie babies.

The fad starts with just a few people. Soon thousands or millions may be doing it. But after a while people lose interest. They start looking for a new fad.

Some fads are toys or games. Back in 1958, schools in Australia used three-foot bamboo rings in gym class. Someone decided to sell these rings as toys. The result was the hula hoop, a large ring that you keep spinning by moving your body. During the summer of 1958, 20 million hula hoops were sold. It was most popular with children who were 5 to 14 years old. Hula hoops were fun and they were great exercise.

Toys called yo-yos were another fad. They were blocks of wood or plastic that moved up and down on a string. A king possessed one in the 17th century. Yo-yos were also once used as weapons by natives in the Philippine Islands. The yo-yo is one fad that returns every 10 or 15 years.

Some fads seem to make no sense at all. Flagpole sitting is an example. Someone sits high above the ground on a tiny platform attached to a tall pole. One 17-year-old girl stayed on her 70 foot tall pole for seven months. Everything she needed was hoisted up to her. It's easy to see why people grew tired of this fad.

(Continued on next page)

Name _____

Fad Fun

(Continued)

      Maybe you like to dance. Just imagine what it would feel like to dance for almost five months with just several short breaks each day! That is the record for marathon dancing, or dancing as long as you can.

      Many of these contests occurred in the 1920's or 1930's. Contestants danced one hour, then enjoyed a 15-minute break. Some dancers fell asleep while their partners kept them moving around the floor. The prize money wouldn't make you rich either. The girl who danced for five months won just $40!

WORDS READ	TIME	WORDS PER MINUTE

1. Name three fads described in the story. _____

2. The hula hoop was an example of a fad that was also _____

3. Why do you think that most fads don't last? _____

4. The record for marathon dancing is how long? _____

5. An example of a fad that doesn't make much sense is _____

Name _____   **Fad Fun**

WORDS

and	few	no	these
be	interest	popular	toys
fad	keep	that	used
fads	king		

Fill in the blanks using the words in the box above.

1. A fad is a certain kind of behavior that is very _____ for a short time.

2. Some _____ were tie dye t-shirts, pet rocks, and beanie babies.

3. The fad starts with just a _____ people.

4. Soon thousands or millions may _____ doing it.

5. But after a while people lose _____ .

6. Some fads are _____ or games.

7. Back in 1958, schools in Australia _____ three-foot bamboo rings in gym class.

8. Someone decided to sell _____ rings as toys.

9. The result was the hula hoop, a large ring that you _____ spinning by moving your body.

10. Hula hoops were fun _____ they were great exercise.

11. Toys called yo-yos were another _____ .

12. A _____ possessed a yo-yo in the 17th century.

13. The yo-yo is one fad _____ returns every 10 or 15 years.

14. Some fads, like flagpole sitting, seem to make _____ sense at all.

©Remedia Publications — 15 — Reading for Speed & Content – Book 3

Name _____

Holidays

WORDS TO KNOW

celebrating	cel • e • brat • ing	groundhog	ground • hog
different	dif • fer • ent	smelly	smell • y
gloomy	gloom • y	special	spe • cial

Holidays

We all know about holidays such as Christmas, Thanksgiving, and 10
the Fourth of July. There are other special days in the year too. This story 25
will tell you about some of those special days. It will also tell you some 40
special facts about holidays. 44

February 2nd is Groundhog Day. The groundhog is a furry little 55
animal who sleeps under the ground in the winter. He comes out in the 69
spring when the weather has warmed up a bit. An old story says that on 84
February 2nd he comes up out of his hole to have a look around. If the 100
sun is shining and he sees his shadow, he scoots back into his hole to 115
sleep for six more weeks. This means winter will last six more weeks. 128

If it's a gloomy day and the groundhog doesn't see his shadow he 141
stays out of his hole and spring comes very soon! Of course, we all know 156
that spring comes on March 21st, groundhog or no groundhog. 166

Another animal has a special day. March 1st is National Pig Day. 178
Many people think pigs are dirty and smelly. They really only seem that 191
way because they often roll in mud. This is how they cool off when it is 207
hot. Pigs are very smart animals. They can be taught to do some of the 222
tricks we teach dogs. So on the next March 1st think some nice thoughts 236
about pigs! 238

The second Sunday in May is Mother's Day. This was made a 250
national holiday by a lady named Anna Jarvis. She spent most of her life 264
taking care of her mother and her sister, who was blind. Anna never 277
married and was never a mother. 283

The third week in October is National Popcorn Week. The United 294

(Continued on next page)

Reading for Speed & Content – Book 3   16   ©Remedia Publications

Name _____   **Holidays**

(Continued)

States grows almost all the popcorn eaten in the whole world. When   306
Columbus came to America, he learned about this strange food from the   318
Indians. Today we can buy popcorn in many, many different flavors. Have 330
you tried Tutti Frutti or Peanut Butter? The average American kid eats   342
about 33 quarts of popcorn each year. Did you know that you can grow   356
popcorn in your yard?   360

    There are many other holidays in the year. Many of them have   372
interesting stories and special reasons for celebrating. The most special, 382
of course, with the best reason, is your birthday!   391

WORDS READ	TIME	WORDS PER MINUTE

1. What day is Groundhog Day? _____

2. What special day comes on March 1st? _____

3. How many children did Anna Jarvis have? _____

4. Where is most of the popcorn grown? _____
   _____

5. How much popcorn does the average kid eat in a year? _____
   _____

6. When is your birthday? __ _____
   _____

Name _____   **Holidays**

WORDS

animal	life	October	second
dirty	named	out	sun
eaten	never	Pigs	taught
holidays			

Fill in the blanks using the words in the box above.

1. The groundhog is a furry little _____ who sleeps under the ground in the winter.

2. He comes _____ in the spring when the weather has warmed up a bit.

3. If the _____ is shining and he sees his shadow, he scoots back into his hole to sleep for six more weeks.

4. Many people think pigs are _____ and smelly.

5. _____ roll in mud to cool off when it is hot.

6. Pigs can be _____ to do some of the tricks we teach dogs.

7. The _____ Sunday in May is Mother's Day.

8. This was made a national holiday by a lady _____ Anna Jarvis.

9. She spent most of her _____ taking care of her mother and her sister, who was blind.

10. Anna _____ married and was never a mother.

11. The third week in _____ is National Popcorn Week.

12. The United States grows almost all the popcorn _____ in the whole world.

13. Many _____ have interesting stories and special reasons for celebrating.

Name _____   ***Funny Fashions***

WORDS TO KNOW

accidentally	ac • ci • den • tal • ly	hairstyles	hair • styles
ancestors	an • ces • tors	lenses	lens • es
ceremonies	cer • e • mo • nies	miners	min • ers
denim	den • im	prevented	pre • vent • ed
enormous	e • nor • mous	scandal	scan • dal
eyeglasses	eye • glass • es	shortened	short • ened

Funny Fashions

Have you ever started to accidentally put your right shoe on your 12
left foot? Of course, you probably didn't get far. That's because each shoe 25
is shaped to fit either your left or right foot, and only that foot. 39

But this wasn't always so. Hundreds of years ago, people wore 50
boots that could cover either foot. 56

Styles of clothes have really changed over the years. The way your 68
ancestors dressed would look pretty odd today! 75

The next time you see a picture of George Washington, check out 87
his clothing. George liked to wear white silk stockings and pants that 99
ended at his knees. He always wore a curly white wig too. Wigs for men 114
were common because they showed the person was important. In fact, the 126
men put on white powder to make them look nicer. 136

Women's hairstyles have changed too. Centuries ago, ladies wore 145
their long hair high up on their heads. They had to sleep sitting up. Often 160
they decorated their hair with feathers or fancy hats that weighed 10 or 15 174
pounds. 175

In those days, American boys had to wear skirts until they were five 188
years old! 190

During the 1700's, English ladies and men had their own kind of 202
designer eyeglasses. They wore the frames without any lenses. The frames 213
were gold and contained jewels. The glasses may have been pretty, but 225
they didn't improve anyone's sight. 230

About 1850, a woman named Amelia Bloomer received lots of 240
attention. She shortened her skirt to just below the knee. That was quite 253

(Continued on next page)

Name _____   **Funny Fashions**

(Continued)

daring. However, she also wore huge, floppy pants under her skirt. That 265
caused a scandal. These oversized pants soon became known as 275
bloomers. 276

    The women who weren't wearing bloomers wore huge skirts that looked 287
like tents. Beneath the skirt was an enormous metal frame holding it in place. 301
It was called a hoop, and it kept ladies from sitting down comfortably. 314

    If men worked outdoors, they bought blue denim jeans called Levi's. 325
The first pairs were made for gold miners in 1849. The pockets were extra 339
sturdy so they could carry gold chunks. 346

    Other countries have their own fashions. Women have always worn 356
pants in Persia and China. Some men in Greece and Scotland still wear 369
skirts. The Scotch call them kilts and they wear them for special 381
ceremonies. 382

WORDS READ	TIME	WORDS PER MINUTE

1. Name a president who wore a wig. _____

2. What did English eyeglasses look like in the 1700's?

   _____

3. Who created huge, floppy pants for women? _____

4. What once held a lady's skirt in place? _____

5. Who were the first pairs of Levi's made for? _____

6. Name two countries where men still wear skirts.

   _____

7. Why do you think shoes are now made to fit the right or left foot only?

   _____

Name _____   **_Funny Fashions_**

WORDS

always	hair	pants	under
boys	known	shoes	would
changed	made	Some	years
for			

Fill in the blanks using the words in the box above.

1. Your _____ are shaped to fit either your left or right foot, and only that foot.

2. Hundreds of _____ ago, people wore boots that could cover either foot.

3. Styles of clothes have really _____ over the years.

4. The way your ancestors dressed _____ look pretty odd today!

5. George Washington liked to wear white silk stockings and _____ that ended at his knees.

6. Wigs _____ men were common because they showed the person was important.

7. Centuries ago, ladies wore their long _____ high up on their heads.

8. In those days, American _____ had to wear skirts until they were five years old!

9. Amelia Bloomer wore huge, floppy pants _____ her skirt.

10. These oversized pants soon became _____ as bloomers.

11. The first pairs of Levi's were _____ for gold miners in 1849.

12. Women have _____ worn pants in Persia and China.

13. _____ men in Greece and Scotland still wear skirts.

©Remedia Publications   21   Reading for Speed & Content – Book 3

Name _____   **Sports Cards**

WORDS TO KNOW

cigarettes	cig • a • rettes	mistake	mis • take
collect	col • lect	season	sea • son
improve	im • prove	tobacco	to • bac • co

Sports Cards

Do you save sports cards? Do you have friends who save them? — 12

The craze for saving these cards with pictures of sports stars on — 24
them started more than 100 years ago! It started with a company called — 37
Old Judge Tobacco Company. — 41

The company printed pictures of baseball players on cardboard. — 50
These were packed with cigarettes to keep them from getting smashed. — 61

Soon, other cigarette companies started doing the same thing. The — 71
pictures were all black and white. Way back then the pictures were all taken — 85
inside. The players would go to a studio. They would pose as if they were — 100
catching a ball. Or they would be swinging at a ball hanging from a string. — 115

In 1933 the cards were printed for bubble gum packages. They were — 127
printed on heavy cardboard and were in color. They had pictures of the — 140
players. They also had tips on how to improve your game. — 151

The idea of sports pictures was a good one. An ice cream company — 164
began printing pictures inside the lids of its ice cream cups. — 175

In 1952 one chewing gum company began adding stories about the — 186
players. — 187

They would tell about the teams they played for and how well they — 200
had done in the past seasons. — 206

A few years later a company started printing All-Star cards. It took a — 220
lot of bubble gum chewing to collect all the All-Stars for each team. — 234

In 1975 a new card called Record Breakers was printed. These — 245
cards had pictures and told about the players who broke records - the — 257
most stolen bases, the most home runs, the most runs batted in. — 269

(Continued on next page)

Name _____   **Sports Cards**

(Continued)

The pictures were taken at spring training each year. The players   280
liked to fool the people who came to take their pictures. One year the bat   295
boy for the California Angels had his picture taken in place of one of the   310
players.   311

The card was printed and packaged with bubble gum. When it was   323
discovered, the card with the "mistake" became very valuable. Some   333
people paid as much as $2 for the "mistake".   342

Many people have huge collections of sports cards and like to trade   354
them with others.   357

WORDS READ	TIME	WORDS PER MINUTE

1. What company first made baseball cards? _____

_____

2. How long ago were the first cards used? _____

3. Name two ways cards have been made better.

_____

_____

4. What was on the Record Breaker cards? _____

_____

5. Whose picture was printed by "mistake"? _____

_____

6. What sports stars, other than baseball, have you seen on cards?

_____

Name _____   **Sports Cards**

WORDS

came	gum	on	the
cards	improve	printed	training
cream	in	sports	valuable

Fill in the blanks using the words in the box above.

1. Do you save _____ cards?

2. The craze for saving these _____ with pictures of sports stars on them started more than 100 years ago!

3. In 1933 the cards were _____ for bubble gum packages.

4. They were printed _____ heavy cardboard and were in color.

5. They also had tips on how to _____ your game.

6. An ice _____ company began printing pictures inside the lids of its ice cream cups.

7. In 1952 one chewing _____ company began adding stories about the players.

8. They would tell about _____ teams they played for and how well they had done in the past seasons.

9. The pictures for the cards were taken at spring _____ each year.

10. The players liked to fool the people who _____ to take their pictures.

11. One year the bat boy for the California Angels had his picture taken _____ place of one of the players.

12. When it was discovered the card with the "mistake" became very _____ .

Name _____   **Film Facts**

WORDS TO KNOW

actress	ac • tress	occasionally	oc • ca • sion • al • ly
cue	cue	phony	pho • ny
eyedropper	eye • drop • per	professional	pro • fes • sion • al
latex	la • tex	recent	re • cent
makeup	make • up	scalp	scalp
material	ma • te • ri • al	wrinkles	wrin • kles

Film Facts

You're watching your favorite TV show. Suddenly, the star begins to cry. You wonder how actresses and actors learn to cry on cue. 11, 23

Well, most actors depend on fake tears. They are put in with an eyedropper just before the scene is filmed. 36, 43

That is one of hundreds of makeup tricks that change people's looks. It's the job of professional makeup artists to make movie faces look a certain way. 54, 67, 70

You've probably seen lots of westerns. Often, someone is shot. Right away red "blood" appears on the screen, yet you know it's not the real thing. But what is it? It's some chemicals that are specially mixed. But unlike real blood, fake blood will not stain, allowing costumes to be washed and worn again. 81, 95, 108, 120, 124

When the role calls for long hair, wigs are used. Occasionally, the role calls for a bald head. Then a skull cap can be glued to the scalp. Years ago, one famous and brave actress chose to shave the top of her head instead. Bette Davis did this to play Queen Elizabeth I of England. 136, 152, 166, 179

Perhaps you've seen an old, old horror movie called "Frankenstein". The monster was a real person with strips of rubber glued to his upper eyelids. This gave him the surprised, dumb look. He also wore black shoe polish on his fingernails. His face was painted blue-green for a deathly look. 189, 203, 216, 229, 230

A more recent movie that turned people into monsters is "Star Wars". The twenty outer space creatures in the famous bar scene are real people. They are wearing special masks like the kind you buy for a 241, 254, 267

(Continued on next page)

©Remedia Publications   25   Reading for Speed & Content – Book 3

Name _____   **Film Facts**

(Continued)

Halloween party. They are made out of a rubber-like material called latex. 280
Holes were cut for breathing and seeing. 287

    The entire mask job was done in just six weeks. At first, the director 301
was disappointed with the results. He thought the creatures looked too 312
phony, but the audience loved it. 318

    In some movies, the star must age many years. Latex is used again 331
to make wrinkles. It is applied in liquid form over the skin, and then 345
powder is used. Very thin, false eyelids are worn over the real ones. 358
Makeup can also create brown age spots or bluish veins that bulge. 370

    It might take five hours to put all this makeup on an actor. To be 385
sure it looks just right, makeup artists practice weeks ahead of time on 398
dummy models. 400

WORDS READ	TIME	WORDS PER MINUTE

1. Name two special effects that are discussed in the story.

   _____
   _____

2. What is the name of the rubber-like material used for masks and to create wrinkles? _____

3. Who was the actress who chose to shave her head? _____

4. What did they do to Frankenstein's eyes to make him look surprised?

   _____
   _____

5. How long does it sometimes take to put all this makeup on an actor?

   _____

Reading for Speed & Content – Book 3   ©Remedia Publications

Name _____   **Film Facts**

WORDS

actors	job	practice	wearing
bald	makeup	space	When
blood	material	tears	with
hours			

Fill in the blanks using the words in the box above.

1. Most actors depend on fake _____ to cry on cue.

2. They are put in _____ an eyedropper just before the scene is filmed.

3. That is one of hundreds of _____ tricks that change people's looks.

4. It's the _____ of professional makeup artists to make movie faces look a certain way.

5. Unlike real blood, fake _____ will not stain, allowing costumes to be washed and worn again.

6. _____ the role calls for long hair, wigs are used.

7. For a _____ head, a skull cap can be glued to the scalp.

8. The twenty outer _____ creatures in the famous bar scene in "Star Wars" are real people.

9. They are _____ special masks like the kind you buy for a Halloween party.

10. They are made out of a rubber-like _____ called latex.

11. Latex is also used to make wrinkles to make _____ look older.

12. It might take five _____ to put all this makeup on an actor.

13. To be sure it looks just right, makeup artists _____ weeks ahead of time on dummy models.

©Remedia Publications   27   Reading for Speed & Content – Book 3

Name _____   *Food for Thought*

WORDS TO KNOW

carnations	car • na • tions	poisonous	poi • son • ous
calories	cal • o • ries	spaghetti	spa • ghet • ti
chopsticks	chop • sticks	thunderstorm	thun • der • storm
explorer	ex • plor • er	varieties	va • ri • e • ties
macaroni	mac • a • ro • ni	vegetables	veg • e • ta • bles
misunderstood	mis • un • der • stood	vinegar	vin • e • gar

Food for Thought

You've probably never eaten Italian spaghetti. You see, it doesn't really come from Italy. It is actually a Chinese dish. The great explorer, Marco Polo, first brought some from China to his home in Italy.

Spaghetti and macaroni are two kinds of food called pasta. Pasta means the food is made from some type of noodle. There are more than 150 varieties of pasta. No one thought to put tomato sauce on pasta for hundreds of years. Instead they used wine as the sauce.

By the way, macaroni really is an Italian dish. It was first made in the 16th century.

Maybe you like mushrooms in your pasta. Lots of people think they taste great, and they are low in calories. Mushrooms have been eaten for thousands of years. The Greeks and Romans thought that thunder made mushrooms. You see, every time there was a big thunderstorm, clumps of mushrooms would appear.

The Egyptians prized mushrooms so much that only their rulers could eat them. The common people were not allowed to sample them.

Unfortunately, some kinds of mushrooms are poisonous. Some well-known kings and popes have died from eating a bad bunch. For years people tried all sorts of home cures, like mixing them with vinegars. At last they gave up. No one in Europe ate them for over a thousand years. But they became popular again during the 16th century.

Speaking of vinegar, it has a long history. Many different flavors were used by the Romans and Greeks. How would you like to try vinegar mixed with pepper, carnations, or mustard? That's what the French did.

(Continued on next page)

Name _____   ***Food for Thought***

(Continued)

    Of course, we know that chop suey is from China. Or is it? The truth 284
is that chop suey was invented in America by a Chinese official. One night 298
he invited a group of his American friends to dinner. They wanted some 311
Chinese food, but he didn't have any in the house. 321

    The man had his cook combine all the vegetables he could find and 334
add soy sauce. Then this new dish was served with chopsticks. All agreed 347
it was delicious. They wanted to know the name of this wonderful Chinese 360
food. 361

    The host looked around and saw the chopsticks and the soy sauce. 373
So he said, "It's called chop-soya." His friends misunderstood and thought 385
he said chop-suey. And that's how a new Chinese-American dish was born. 399

WORDS READ	TIME	WORDS PER MINUTE

1. What country did spaghetti come from? _____

2. Name two kinds of pasta. _____
   _____

3. The Greeks thought that mushrooms came from _____ .

4. The French used pepper, carnations, and mustard to flavor _____

5. An American dish invented by a Chinese official is _____ .

6. Chop suey gets it name from these two things: _____
   _____

7. If you found mushrooms growing in a forest, would it be a good idea to taste them? Why or why not? _____
   _____

©Remedia Publications   Reading for Speed & Content – Book 3

Name _____   *Food for Thought*

WORDS

all	different	invented	one
and	eaten	macaroni	pasta
called	explorer	mushrooms	poisonous
Chinese			

Fill in the blanks using the words in the box above.

1. The great _____, Marco Polo, first brought spaghetti from China to his home in Italy.

2. Spaghetti and _____ are two kinds of food called pasta.

3. There are more than 150 varieties of _____ .

4. No _____ thought to put tomato sauce on pasta for hundreds of years.

5. Mushrooms have been _____ for thousands of years.

6. The Greeks _____ Romans thought that thunder made mushrooms.

7. The Egyptians prized _____ so much that only their rulers could eat them.

8. Unfortunately, some kinds of mushrooms are _____ .

9. Many _____ flavors of vinegar were used by the Romans and Greeks.

10. Chop suey was _____ in America by a Chinese official.

11. His American friends wanted some _____ food, but he didn't have any in the house.

12. So he had his cook combine _____ the vegetables he could find and add soy sauce.

13. He said, "It's _____ chop-soya."

Reading for Speed & Content – Book 3   ©Remedia Publications

Name _____

A Castle Fit for a Vampire

WORDS TO KNOW

century	cen • tu • ry	remodeled	re • mod • eled
furnishings	fur • nish • ings	reputation	rep • u • ta • tion
kingdom	king • dom	vampire	vam • pire
passageway	pas • sage • way	vaulted	vault • ed

A Castle Fit for a Vampire

Partly hidden among some mountains in Romania there lies a huge 11
stone castle. Bran Castle is believed to have once been the home of the 25
horrible Prince Vlad Dracula. Dracula lived from 1431 to 1476. His 36
reputation for evil is told in legends, for he killed many people. 48

Bran Castle is well preserved. It contains lots of rooms with vaulted 60
ceilings. Some of the doors have arches. There is even a secret 72
passageway, perhaps for quick escapes. 77

On the lower level there is a prison. It is thought that the Prince was 92
once jailed here when he made the king angry. At the top of the castle are 108
pointed towers. Soldiers stood guard there. They hurled rocks and 118
poured boiling water on any enemies who attacked Bran Castle. 128

Prince Dracula was made famous by an Irish writer named Bram 139
Stoker. He wrote a book in the 1890's called Dracula. The name means 152
"devil's son." Stoker described Dracula's home as "...a vast ruined castle, 163
from whose tall black windows came no ray of light." The castle was 176
located near a kingdom called Transylvania. 182

The main character in his book was inspired by the evil deeds of the 196
Prince. But there was at least one difference. Stoker made his Dracula a 209
vampire. That is a creature who sucks blood from his victims. It only 222
comes out at night. In real life, we know that there are no such things as 238
human vampires. But there are plenty of stories about them. Many 249
movies have been made from Stoker's book. 256

It is worth knowing that Stoker never even saw Romania or Bran 268
Castle. He found all his facts by reading books at the library. Yet he 282

(Continued on next page)

©Remedia Publications   31   Reading for Speed & Content – Book 3

Name _____   **A Castle Fit for a Vampire**

(Continued)

brought this feared person back to life. He did this through the pages of   296
his book.   298
    Bran Castle has had some interesting owners over the centuries. In   309
the 1930's it was the favorite summer home of Queen Marie. She   321
remodeled the castle and chose new furnishings which are still used   332
today. One thing is for sure. Queen Marie was not afraid to live in a home   348
that might have been owned by a vampire!   356

WORDS READ	TIME	WORDS PER MINUTE

1. Bran Castle is located in the country of _____ .

2. How did the soldiers try to keep enemies away from Bran Castle?

   _____

   _____

3. How did Prince Dracula become famous hundreds of years after he died?

   _____

   _____

4. How did Bram Stoker learn about Prince Dracula?

   _____

   _____

5. Are there really human vampires? _____

Name _____

A Castle Fit for a Vampire

WORDS

among	brought	never	there
believed	famous	owners	vampire
blood	horrible	reading	wrote
book			

Fill in the blanks using the words in the box above.

1. Partly hidden _____ some mountains in Romania there lies a huge stone castle.

2. Bran Castle is _____ to have once been the home of the evil Prince Vlad Dracula.

3. Prince Dracula was made _____ by an Irish writer named Bram Stoker.

4. He _____ a book in the 1890's called Dracula.

5. The main character in his book was inspired by the _____ deeds of the Prince.

6. But Stoker also made his Dracula a _____ .

7. A vampire is a creature who sucks _____ from his victims.

8. In real life, we know that _____ are no such things as human vampires.

9. It is worth knowing that Stoker _____ even saw Romania or Bran Castle.

10. He found all his facts by _____ books at the library.

11. Yet he _____ this feared person back to life.

12. He did this through the pages of his _____ .

13. Bran Castle has had some interesting _____ over the centuries.

Name _____

Smokey the Bear

WORDS TO KNOW

advertising	ad • ver • tis • ing	message	mes • sage
campfire	camp • fire	prevent	pre • vent
destroyed	de • stroyed	prevention	pre • ven • tion
equipment	e • quip • ment	symbol	sym • bol

Smokey the Bear

Smokey the Bear began as an advertising idea over 60 years ago. In 1942 the men who worked in the forests in California were worried about the number of fires destroying the forests.

They did not have the money or the people to do a good job of fighting forest fires. They did not have enough equipment either. They had an idea.

If they could find a way to remind people to be more careful, maybe the number of fires would be less. Many artists and writers worked on ideas. None of them seemed just right.

At last, in 1945, everyone agreed that an animal should be used. If the animal they chose could stand upright, it could use its paws and front legs to show ways to prevent forest fires.

Of course, a bear seemed just perfect.

A well-known artist, Albert Staehel, was asked to draw the bear. He drew the bear wearing overalls and an old style ranger's hat. The very first poster showed the bear pouring water over a campfire. It said, "Smokey says - Care will prevent 9 out of 10 forest fires."

The friendly bear became a well-known character to millions of Americans. They paid attention to Smokey's messages. Very soon the number of forest fires became less.

Smokey was seen on posters, bumper stickers, and in magazines and newspapers. His message was always the same: "Take care of our wonderful forests."

In 1950 a tiny black bear cub was rescued from a forest fire in New

(Continued on next page)

Reading for Speed & Content – Book 3   34   ©Remedia Publications

Name _____   ***Smokey the Bear***

(Continued)

Mexico. He was badly burned. He was cared for by a girl named Judy Bill.   268
Her father was the game warden of New Mexico. Judy and her father   281
named the baby cub Smokey.   286

    When Smokey was well he was flown on an airplane to Washington,   298
D.C. The National Zoo in Washington became his home. He was a living   311
symbol of forest fire prevention.   316

    On November 9, 1977, Smokey the Bear died at the National Zoo.   328
His body was taken to the Smokey Bear State Park in New Mexico.   341

    Smokey's messages are still seen and heard in forests and parks all   353
over America.   355

WORDS READ	TIME	WORDS PER MINUTE

1. Why were the forest workers in California worried? _____

2. Why was a bear used? _____

3. What was Smokey's first message? _____

4. How did Smokey's messages help? _____

5. Who helped save the bear cub? _____

Name _____ **Smokey the Bear**

WORDS

agreed	could	not	perfect
artists	drew	less	to
asked	forests	people	water
began			

Fill in the blanks using the words in the box above.

1. Smokey the Bear _____ as an advertising idea over 60 years ago.

2. The men who worked in the _____ in California were worried about the number of fires destroying the forests.

3. They did _____ have the money or the people to do a good job of fighting forest fires.

4. If they could find a way to remind _____ to be more careful maybe the number of fires would be less.

5. Many _____ and writers worked on ideas.

6. Everyone _____ that an animal should be used.

7. If the animal they chose could stand upright, it _____ use its paws and front legs to show ways to prevent forest fires.

8. Of course, a bear seemed just _____ .

9. A well-known artist, Albert Staehel, was _____ to draw the bear.

10. He _____ the bear wearing overalls and an old style ranger's hat.

11. The very first poster showed the bear pouring _____ over a campfire.

12. Americans paid attention _____ Smokey's messages.

13. Very soon the number of forest fires became _____ .

Reading for Speed & Content – Book 3   36   ©Remedia Publications

Name _____

Amazing Artists

WORDS TO KNOW

gallery	gal • ler • y	imagination	i • mag • i • na • tion
braille	(bray • ul)	musician	mu • si • cian
cockroach	cock • roach	orchestra	or • ches • tra
conducted	con • duct • ed	published	pub • lished

Amazing Artists

    The artists in this story are amazing for a very special reason. Some 13
were artists, some writers, and some musicians. Not so amazing? They 24
were all children! 27

    In 1933, a young lady named Margaret Heifetz conducted the 37
Moscow Orchestra in Russia. Margaret was 9 years old. 46

    Alfred Cohen had his art on display. Many people read about it in 59
the newspaper. They came to see his work. He had 40 paintings on 72
display. Alfred was only 8 years old. 79

    William Marsh, at age 11, wrote and had published the story of the 92
life of President Herbert Hoover. 97

    Philippa Schuyler was a very talented young lady. At the age of 2½ 110
she could spell 550 words. One of those words was rhinoceros! She loved 123
music. At age 6 she wrote a piece called "Cockroach Ballet." When she 136
was 13 she played the piano with a 100-piece symphony orchestra as 149
they played the music she had written. 156

    Jimmy Boyd was only 12 when he made the hit record, "I Saw 169
Mommy Kissing Santa Claus." He earned $100,000 from that one song. 180

    A book titled *How the World Began* was published in 1964. Its 192
author, Dorothy Straight, was only 4 years old! 200

    A 12 year old, Janet Lessing, had her paintings on display in a Los 214
Angeles art gallery. They sold for $50 and $100. What made Janet even 227
more amazing was that she was almost blind. Because she didn't see well 240
she often created worlds in her imagination. She could see just fine there! 253

    Shirley Temple, the famous child movie star, began making movies 263

(Continued on next page)

Name _____   **Amazing Artists**

(Continued)

when she was 7 years old. She was getting 5,000 letters a week from people 278
who loved her movies. 282

    We all have heard of Louis Braille, who invented an alphabet for the 295
blind. He had been blind since he was 3, and he was only 15 years old when 312
he finished his special alphabet to help others. 320

    All these amazing young people have given something special for others 331
to share. 333

WORDS READ	TIME	WORDS PER MINUTE

1. Who wrote the life story of a president? _____

2. What was the name of Miss Schuyler's ballet? _____

3. What song earned a lot of money for a 12-year-old? _____

4. What made artist Janet Lessing even more amazing? _____

5. How old was Louis Braille when he lost his sight? _____

6. Do you have a special talent? _____

Name _____   *Amazing Artists*

WORDS

alphabet	book	hit	she
amazing	called	orchestra	wrote
artists	display	others	

Fill in the blanks using the words in the box above.

1. The artists in this story are _____ for a very special reason.

2. Some were _____, some writers, and some musicians, and they were all children!

3. Nine-year-old Margaret Heifetz conducted the Moscow _____ in Russia.

4. Alfred Cohen had his art on _____ when he was only 8 years old.

5. William Marsh, at age 11, _____ and had published the story of the life of President Herbert Hoover.

6. Philippa Schuyler loved music and wrote a piece _____ "Cockroach Ballet" at age 6.

7. When Philippa was 13, _____ played the piano with a 100-piece symphony orchestra as they played the music she had written.

8. Jimmy Boyd was only 12 when he made the _____ record, "I Saw Mommy Kissing Santa Claus."

9. Four-year-old Dorothy Straight wrote a _____ titled "How the World Began."

10. Louis Braille invented an _____ for the blind.

11. All these amazing young people have given something special for _____ to share.

Name _____ **Teddy Bears**

WORDS TO KNOW

cartoonist	car • toon • ist	jointed	joint • ed
defenseless	de • fense • less	nephew	neph • ew
dressmaker	dress • mak • er	shopkeeper	shop • keep • er

Teddy Bears

    Do you have a Teddy Bear? Most children have grown up with at least one, if not many. These cute, cuddly, stuffed toys have been popular ever since they were created over 100 years ago! Who had the idea for this wonderful toy?

    The name comes from the 26th President of the United States, Theodore "Teddy" Roosevelt. President Roosevelt liked to hunt. One day in 1902 he was on a bear hunting trip, but couldn't find one. Finally, other people in the hunting party found a bear and tied it to a tree. But Roosevelt refused to shoot the defenseless animal. The next day, a cartoonist drew a picture of the president refusing to kill the bear. It was published in many newspapers across the country.

    When Morris Michtom, a shopkeeper in Brooklyn, New York, heard this story, he got an idea. He asked his wife to make two plush stuffed bears to put in his shop's display window. He asked for and received permission from Roosevelt himself to call them "Teddy's Bears." The bears were an instant success. They later became known simply as Teddy Bears (without the "s" after Teddy).

    Before then, bear toys looked more like real bears – they were fierce looking and stood on all fours. But the Teddy Bears were cute and stood upright, more like people.

    Michtom wasn't the only one to come up with the idea for this kind of bear. Margarete Steiff, a dressmaker in Germany, had started a business making all kinds of stuffed animals. She used drawings that her nephew had made of bear cubs at a zoo to make a toy bear. It was jointed

(Continued on next page)

Name _____ **Teddy Bears**

(Continued)

like dolls and stood upright. 281

    In 1903 the Steiff Company introduced its bear at a trade fair for 294
people who buy toys to sell in shops. An American was there and thought 308
the German toy was a lot like the Teddy Bears that were popular in the 323
United States. So he placed an order for 3,000 Steiff bears. By the end of 338
the year he ordered 12,000! 343

    Today Teddy Bears are still popular and much-loved by children 354
everywhere. Adults often collect them. They come in all shapes, colors, and 366
sizes. Few toys have such a long history, or such an interesting beginning! 379

WORDS READ	TIME	WORDS PER MINUTE

1. How long have Teddy Bears been around? _____

2. What president is the Teddy Bear named after? _____

3. How were Teddy Bears different from other bear toys? _____

4. What were Teddy Bears first called? _____

5. Who was the shopkeeper in Brooklyn who sold Teddy Bears? _____

6. Where else were Teddy Bears made? _____

7. Describe your favorite Teddy Bear. _____

Name _____   **Teddy Bears**

WORDS

bear	from	make	refused
business	hunting	next	the
found	idea	President	who

Fill in the blanks using the words in the box above.

1. The name Teddy Bear comes from the 26th _____ of the United States, Theodore "Teddy" Roosevelt.

2. One day President Roosevelt was on a bear _____ trip, but couldn't find one.

3. Finally, other people in the hunting party _____ a bear and tied it to a tree.

4. But Roosevelt _____ to shoot the defenseless animal.

5. The _____ day, a cartoonist drew a picture of the president refusing to kill the bear.

6. When Morris Michtom, a shopkeeper in Brooklyn, New York, heard this story, he got an _____ .

7. He asked his wife to _____ two plush stuffed bears to put in his shop's display window.

8. He asked for and received permission _____ Roosevelt himself to call them "Teddy's Bears".

9. Michtom wasn't the only one to come up with the idea for this kind of _____ .

10. Margarete Steiff, a dressmaker in Germany, had started a _____ making all kinds of stuffed animals.

11. In 1903 the Steiff Company introduced its bear at a trade fair for people _____ buy toys to sell in shops.

12. An American was there and thought _____ German toy was a lot like the Teddy Bears that were popular in the United States.

Timed Reading Chart

TO FIND WORDS PER MINUTE:
1) Find the number of words read across the top of the chart.
2) Find the time in minutes/seconds down the left side of the chart.
3) The intersection of the two will give the words per minute.

TOTAL WORDS READ

TIME	200	205	210	215	220	225	230	235	240	245	250	255	260	265	270	275	280	285	290	295
2:00	100	103	105	108	110	113	115	118	120	123	125	128	130	133	135	138	140	143	145	148
2:05	96	99	101	103	106	108	110	113	115	117	120	122	124	127	129	131	134	136	138	141
2:10	92	95	97	99	102	104	106	108	111	113	115	118	120	122	125	127	129	131	133	135
2:15	89	91	93	96	98	100	102	14	107	109	111	113	115	118	120	122	124	126	129	131
2:20	86	88	90	92	94	96	98	101	103	105	107	109	111	113	116	118	120	122	124	126
2:25	83	85	87	89	91	93	95	97	99	101	103	105	107	109	112	114	116	118	120	122
2:30	80	82	84	96	88	90	92	94	96	98	100	102	104	106	108	110	112	114	116	118
2:35	77	79	81	93	85	87	89	91	93	95	97	99	101	103	105	107	109	111	113	115
2:40	75	77	79	81	83	85	87	89	91	93	95	97	98	99	101	103	105	107	109	111
2:45	73	75	76	78	80	82	84	85	87	89	91	93	95	96	98	100	12	104	106	107
2:50	71	73	74	76	78	79	81	83	85	86	88	90	92	94	95	97	99	101	102	104
2:55	69	71	72	74	75	77	79	81	82	84	86	88	89	91	93	95	96	98	100	102
3:00	67	69	70	72	73	75	77	78	80	82	83	85	87	88	90	92	93	95	97	98
3:05	65	67	68	70	71	73	75	76	78	79	81	83	84	86	88	89	91	92	94	96
3:10	63	65	66	68	69	71	73	74	76	77	79	81	82	84	85	87	88	90	92	93
3:15	62	63	65	66	68	69	71	72	74	75	77	78	80	81	83	84	86	88	89	91
3:20	60	62	63	65	66	68	69	71	72	74	75	77	78	80	81	83	84	86	87	89
3:25	59	60	61	63	64	66	67	69	70	72	73	75	76	78	79	80	82	83	85	96
3:30	57	59	60	61	63	64	66	67	69	70	71	73	74	76	77	79	80	81	83	84

TOTAL WORDS READ

TIME	300	305	310	315	320	325	330	335	340	345	350	355	360	365	370	375	380	385	390	395	400
2:00	150	153	155	158	160	163	165	168	170	173	175	177	180	182	185	188	190	192	195	197	200
2:05	143	145	148	150	152	155	157	159	162	165	168	170	173	175	178	180	182	185	187	190	192
2:10	138	140	142	145	147	149	152	154	156	159	162	164	166	168	171	173	175	178	180	182	185
2:15	133	135	137	140	142	144	146	148	151	153	156	158	160	162	164	167	169	171	173	176	178
2:20	128	131	133	135	137	139	141	143	146	148	150	152	154	156	159	161	163	165	167	169	171
2:25	124	126	128	130	132	134	137	139	141	143	145	147	149	151	153	155	157	159	161	163	166
2:30	120	122	124	126	128	130	132	134	136	138	140	142	144	146	148	150	152	154	156	158	160
2:35	117	119	121	123	125	127	129	131	133	134	135	137	139	141	143	145	147	149	151	153	155
2:40	113	114	116	118	120	122	124	126	128	129	131	133	135	137	139	141	143	144	146	148	150
2:45	109	111	113	115	117	118	120	122	124	125	127	129	131	133	135	136	138	140	142	144	145
2:50	106	108	110	111	113	115	117	118	120	122	124	125	127	129	131	132	134	136	138	139	141
2:55	103	105	107	109	110	111	113	115	117	118	120	122	123	125	127	129	130	132	134	135	137
3:00	100	102	103	105	107	108	110	112	113	115	117	118	120	122	123	125	127	128	130	132	133
3:05	97	99	101	102	104	105	107	109	110	112	114	115	117	118	120	122	123	125	126	128	130
3:10	95	96	98	99	101	103	104	106	107	109	111	112	114	115	117	118	120	122	123	125	126
3:15	92	94	95	97	98	100	101	103	104	106	108	109	111	112	114	115	117	118	120	122	123
3:20	90	92	93	95	96	98	99	101	103	140	105	107	108	110	111	113	114	116	117	119	120
3:25	88	89	91	92	94	95	97	98	100	101	102	104	105	107	108	110	111	113	114	116	117
3:30	86	87	89	90	91	93	94	96	97	99	100	101	103	104	106	107	109	110	111	113	114

©Remedia Publications

Reading for Speed & Content – Book 3

Keeping Track

Name _____

Date	Story Title	No. of words in story	No. of words read	Time in minutes & seconds	Words per minute	Questions correct
	Chewing Gum	338				
	Band-Aids	343				
	Kids' Railroad	338				
	Think Ink	339				
	Fad Fun	390				
	Holidays	391				
	Funny Fashions	382				
	Sports Cards	357				
	Film Facts	400				
	Food for Thought	399				
	A Castle Fit for a Vampire	356				
	Smokey the Bear	355				
	Amazing Artists	333				
	Teddy Bears	379				

Reading for Speed & Content – Book 3 ©Remedia Publications

Answer Key

PG#

2 1) chicle 2) the sapodilla tree in Mexico 3) a new kind of rubber or false teeth "glue" 4) flavoring and sugar 5) in big, flat sheets 6) He spent more money on ads. 7) *Answers will vary* 8) Because it is better for your teeth (*answers may vary*)

3 1) chewing 2) Chicle 3) tried 4) it 5) sold 6) Shopkeepers 7) would 8) companies 9) more 10) America 11) colors 12) choose 13) around

5 1) Johnson and Johnson 2) because she had many small cuts 3) It made it faster for her to fix her cuts. 4) because it belongs to Johnson and Johnson 5) about 4 billion 6) plastic tape

6 1) man 2) scrapes 3) wife 4) time 5) over 6) she 7) had 8) accident 9) what 10) thought 11) wrapper 12) better

8 1) so they can play with them 2) Pioneer Railway 3) about 50 4) 7 miles long 5) people's lives depend on safety 6) more than 30 years 7) Between the ages of 10-14, do very well in school, past tests, go to special classes

9 1) invented 2) play 3) unusual 4) children 5) duty 6) sellers 7) all 8) forth 9) it 10) goes 11) to 12) months 13) seriously

11 1) 4,500 years ago 2) Egypt and China 3) quills 4) the ballpoint pen 5) blue, black, red 6) invisible ink 7) blue 8) *Answers will vary*

12 1) liquid 2) ink 3) wrote 4) years 5) sticks 6) major 7) had 8) make 9) red 10) long 11) ballpoint 12) stay 13) Invisible 14) blue

14 1) *Answers will vary* 2) good exercise 3) people get tired of them (*answers may vary*) 4) 5 months 5) flagpole sitting

15 1) popular 2) fads 3) few 4) be 5) interest 6) toys 7) used 8) these 9) keep 10) and 11) fad 12) king 13) that 14) no

17 1) February 2 2) National Pig Day 3) none 4) United States 5) 33 quarts 6) *Answers will vary*

18 1) animal 2) out 3) sun 4) dirty 5) Pigs 6) taught 7) second 8) named 9) life 10) never 11) October 12) eaten 13) holidays

20 1) George Washington 2) no lenses; gold and jewels 3) Amelia Bloomer 4) hoops 5) gold miners 6) Greece & Scotland 7) So they are more comfortable (*answers may vary*)

21 1) shoes 2) years 3) changed 4) would 5) pants 6) for 7) hair 8) boys 9) under 10) known 11) made

PG#

12) always 13) some

23 1) Old Judge Tobacco Co. 2) 100 years ago 3) They are on heavy cardboard and in color. 4) players who broke records 5) California Angels' batboy 6) football, hockey (*answers may vary*)

24 1) sports 2) cards 3) printed 4) on 5) improve 6) cream 7) gum 8) the 9) training 10) came 11) in 12) valuable

26 1) crying, blood, wigs/skull caps, masks, aging (*answers will vary*) 2) latex 3) Bette Davis 4) glued rubber to his eyelids 5) 5 hours

27 1) tears 2) with 3) makeup 4) job 5) blood 6) When 7) bald 8) space 9) wearing 10) material 11) actors 12) hours 13) practice

29 1) China 2) spaghetti, macaroni (*answers will vary*) 3) thunder 4) vinegar 5) chop suey 6) chopsticks and soy sauce 7) No, because some kinds are poisonous.

30 1) explorer 2) macaroni 3) pasta 4) one 5) eaten 6) and 7) mushrooms 8) poisonous 9) different 10) invented 11) Chinese 12) all 13) called

32 1) Romania 2) threw stones and boiling water 3) Bram Stoker wrote a book about him. 4) He read about him. 5) No

33 1) among 2) believed 3) famous 4) wrote 5) horrible 6) vampire 7) blood 8) there 9) never 10) reading 11) brought 12) book 13) owners

35 1) There were many fires. 2) It can stand upright. 3) Care will prevent 9 out of 10 forest fires. 4) people paid attention 5) Judy Bill

36 1) began 2) forests 3) not 4) people 5) artists 6) agreed 7) could 8) perfect 9) asked 10) drew 11) water 12) to 13) less

38 1) William Marsh 2) Cockroach Ballet 3) I Saw Mommy Kissing Santa Claus 4) She was almost blind. 5) 3 years old 6) *Answers will vary*

39 1) amazing 2) artists 3) orchestra 4) display 5) wrote 6) called 7) she 8) hit 9) book 10) alphabet 11) others

41 1) 100 years 2) Theodore Roosevelt 3) They were cute and stood upright like people. 4) Teddy's Bears 5) Morris Michtom 6) Germany 7) *Answers will vary*

42 1) President 2) hunting 3) found 4) refused 5) next 6) idea 7) make 8) from 9) bear 10) business 11) who 12) the

©Remedia Publications

Reading for Speed & Content – Book 3